# ECONOMICS OR POLITICS?

# ECONOMICS
## OR
# POLITICS?

*A lecture by*

PAUL VAN ZEELAND

formerly Prime Minister
of Belgium

*Delivered at Cambridge*
*17 October 1938*

CAMBRIDGE
AT THE UNIVERSITY PRESS
1939

# CAMBRIDGE
## UNIVERSITY PRESS

University Printing House, Cambridge CB2 8BS, United Kingdom

Published in the United States of America by Cambridge University Press, New York

Cambridge University Press is part of the University of Cambridge.

It furthers the University's mission by disseminating knowledge in the pursuit of education, learning and research at the highest international levels of excellence.

www.cambridge.org
Information on this title: www.cambridge.org/9781107637344

© Cambridge University Press 1939

First published 1939
First paperback edition 2014

*A catalogue record for this publication is available from the British Library*

ISBN 978-1-107-63734-4 Paperback

# CONTENTS AND ANALYSIS

( 5 )

B. Examination of difficulties inherent in international economic relations, and which must be taken into account in the preparing of a solution.

(1) The need for "fair play"—for development in both directions, in imports as in exports.

(2) The effects of changes of economic and social structure.

(3) Fundamental inequalities in the conditions of competition.

(4) The need for securing a sufficiently long period of adjustment.

(5) Legitimate concern for national security and for economic and social stability.

(6) Monetary aspects of the problem.

III. Examination of the practical means of realisation.

    A. A moderate solution: limit deterioration and stop its extension.

    A step towards a far-reaching reorganisation, which can only result from measures taken in the national field.

    B. The urgency of the problem and the need for immediate initiative.

    Agreement open to all: Ouchy type. The will to advance?

    C. Whence can come the initiative?

Conclusion.

# I. INTRODUCTION

Will you allow me to say a few words by way of introduction? Never have I been at such a loss in preparing a lecture as I have been on this occasion. To speak at Cambridge is a privilege, but also a responsibility. You form here one of the most distinguished homes of scientific life in England. I hesitated a long while as to whether I should work out before you, with the objectiveness of a piece of research, some intricate problem of economic science. But I reflected that you form as well a centre of intellectual and moral enlightenment. In the exceptionally troubled days in which we live, it may be as useful to draw the attention of well-informed opinion to some problems that have been brought forward, as to do the work of a pioneer in scientific fields that are as yet unexplored.

I am going, therefore, to speak to you of problems of very present interest, which arise at the point where politics and economics meet. I shall tell you nothing that you do not already know. I shall try to avoid figures and statistics. I shall, above all, appeal to common sense. But from the sort of self-examination which I propose that we make together, there will perhaps result some practical conclusions, of which the effect may serve—directly or indirectly—the cause of real peace.

I was concerned a short while ago with the drafting of a Report on the possibility of reducing the obstacles to international trade. The initiative, which ultimately resulted in this Report, came from the British and French governments. It was the expression of the determination, or at least of the desire, of the leaders of those two countries to break the vicious circle in which international economic activity had been so long enclosed.

The reception given to the suggestions of this Report was, in my opinion, quite revealing. It corresponded essentially to the "atmosphere" which my collaborator and myself had encountered in the various capitals on the occasion of the contacts that we had made in the preparing of the Report.

Indeed, the general lines of the Report, as well as the "tendency" to which the suggestions made are linked, have been comparatively well received in the majority of countries. The objections that have been made have been concerned either with points of detail, or with questions of expediency, or again with the moderate and conservative nature of the solutions outlined. Nowhere, as far as I know, has criticism taken the form of a refutation of the principles and aspirations on which the Report is based. Nowhere has a counter-solution been put forward, a solution pointing in a different direction and based either on autarkic conceptions or on radical and absolute free trade, or on a rigid organisation of international economic relations, under the authority of the particular states.

Yet, despite the initial determination of two great powers, despite the understanding and favourable attitude of several others, despite the benevolent neutrality of the majority of the countries of the world towards a new effort, we are still in "no man's land". Nearly two years have passed since the initiative was taken. It will soon be ten months since the Report was handed over to those for whom it was destined. The curve of economic activity has, since then, twice changed direction; it was first directed upwards, then it fell and took a downward turn, then it checked its course and for the moment it is almost horizontal....I do not want to speak about the evolution of political conditions. But this I may say, with the agreement, I suppose, of everyone: The need for an international reorganisation, and the desire for a new factor which might direct the destinies of the world into other channels, have become ever more imperative. Yet, despite everything, no step of any kind has hitherto been taken towards a better international economic collaboration.

For such a static attitude, for this inertia, which each individual seems to condemn and regret, but to which everyone seems in fact to cling, there must be reasons. Let us try to discover them. We may then see whether it is possible to overcome or circumvent the difficulties to which these reasons correspond.

## II

## OBSTACLES
## TO A REORGANISATION OF
## INTERNATIONAL ECONOMIC
## RELATIONS

### A. EXTERNAL OBJECTIONS

(1) *Existing Political Difficulties*

You have often heard it said, before Munich and after it, that "in existing political conditions, there is nothing to be done from the economic point of view". Put that way, the problem is wrongly stated, and there is a danger of its being insoluble. Of course, in an atmosphere of virtual war, it would be vain to evoke ways and means of international collaboration. If certain leaders had their minds firmly made up to war, it is clear that they would brush aside anything that would tend to bring the nations closer together.

But do the facts present themselves in this way? I do not know. But I refuse, for myself, to believe that there are in the world responsible leaders who desire war for its own sake.

( 14 )

Even those whom we regard as actuated by a dangerous spirit probably contemplate a resort to violence as a last extremity only. The real danger is that certain of them, caught between threatening and contradictory difficulties, may, at a certain point, perceive in war a possible way out, and may choose to run the risk of a bloody adventure.

What we must seek is the means of solving those difficulties, if we can, so as to suppress immediate risks of war. Approached from that angle, economic preoccupations once more become of primary importance.

Doubtless material difficulties or considerations do not comprise the whole of politics. Of this the anxious weeks that Europe has just passed through under the cloud of the Czechoslovakian problem are a living proof. Feelings, passions, ambitions, ideologies that have nothing to do with the economic well-being of citizens, play in the conduct of public affairs a part that is never negligible and sometimes preponderant. The totalitarian systems are based on sentiment, not on reason; all their propaganda appeals to passions, never to reasoning. Hence, it is not surprising that our age comes up against problems which far surpass the concepts of political economy.

Nevertheless, when we look closely into the facts, we become once more aware of the intimate connection between economic and political considerations; it is virtually impossible to find an economic problem which is not complicated by political aspects, and the political questions to which economic preoccupations are not directly or indirectly linked are rare indeed. In point of fact, we find ourselves, usually, confronted by a complex of difficulties, composed of political, economic and social elements mingled inextricably together.

From what direction must this great problem be approached? I should like to reply: From anywhere, provided that a start is made! Do not let us acquiesce in doing nothing, by taking refuge behind the convenient but artificial screen of so-called insurmountable political difficulties.

## (2) *Autarky or International Economics*

Another question at once comes to one's mind. In trying to develop economic relations on the international plane, are we in the right? Would it not be better to turn resolutely in the other direction, and reduce to the strict minimum these international exchanges, which prove to be so difficult, and the source of so many conflicts?

The question seems to me answered by facts, independently of any theoretical research. I do not know of any period in the history of Europe when more obstacles—more skilful and more effective ones—have been accumulated against international trade. And yet, the volume of this trade has been maintained at a relatively high level. According to the League of Nations Department of Economic Studies, international trade in 1937 represented, in gold value, more than three-quarters (0·77) as regards imports, and almost four-fifths as regards exports, of the figures for 1913. The "quantum" of international trade, so far as concerns imports, was 5 per cent higher in 1937 than ten years before.

Even those countries which, for reasons of principle or expediency, have made the most vigorous and deliberate efforts towards an autarkic system, have had no choice but to continue with the rest of the world economic relations which are not very much below the level of those existing before the War. In 1935 the imports and exports of Germany, in metric tons, were about two-thirds of those of 1913; Russia exported in 1935 about three-quarters of what she exported in 1913. The "quantum" of the exports of Italy in 1937 was one-fifth higher than in 1925. Could one find a more obvious proof of the necessity of international trade? The conclusion is that, in practice, one cannot do without it.

At this point, an ironical critic might object: But if international trade is in a relatively healthy condition, are you not tilting against windmills? Let things go on as they are, they will recover by themselves, since there is a need for them.

No, the situation is not satisfactory. The water is trickling through the dams, and in the end it becomes a current. But what a waste of power! What a stupid loss of energy! What a sum of uncertainties, deceptions and injustices, individual and collective! Those who, in these troubled times, enter upon the winding paths of international trade, must develop an energy, a skill, a suppleness which would be a thousand times more useful elsewhere. Besides, the risks that they run are so great that they cannot but think enviously on occasion of the sword of Damocles.

Moreover, if those relations which are absolutely indispensable are thus formed amid countless obstacles and risks, think of the immense difference separating what is from what ought to be or might be. Think of the tremendous assistance that each national economic system would receive from an international system functioning normally, with a volume of business worthy of the progress that has been made in the technique of production and transport.

The present situation is therefore not satisfactory. If it is not still worse, one may say that that is not the fault of men; they have done about all they could to render business impossible. They have not succeeded in stifling it entirely. But the situation that has been created is bristling with unnecessary difficulties; disorganisation goes on increasing; a thousand possibilities remain unutilised, and all the political consequences that are concealed behind economic disequilibria lie there like a smouldering fire.

Since international trade is an unavoidable necessity, since it goes on, despite obstacles and confusion, does not the most immediate and empirical wisdom prescribe that it should be regulated, organised, and at least given a sufficient degree of clarity, stability, suppleness and freedom of action? From this point of view it seems to me that no one can refuse to collaborate, whatever may be his theoretical standpoint, his preferences, his grievances or his ambitions.

## (3) *Ideological Differences and their Relation to International Trade*

Are there, with regard to international economic activity, two opposed points of view, based on different ideological conceptions? In particular, are the violent oppositions, which trace a clear-cut line between political conceptions based on the totalitarian state and those characteristic of representative government, extended into this particular domain of economics?

The reply to this question is less simple than appears at first sight. Doubtless, the internal logic of a totalitarian movement, with a nationalist or race basis, does not stop at the ill-defined boundaries of economics. As soon as one admits the principle—a false one, but clear—which is the sole foundation of these movements, then any limitation, any frontier which is not that of the nation or of the race, is condemned to disappearance.

The power of the state, incarnated in the chief, is absolute: it is as much or more so in the economic field as in the cultural, religious or moral field.

The race, the nation, must form a complete unit. Remember the motto: Ein Volk, ein Staat, ein Führer! Has that any meaning without economic independence? From thence to autarky it is but a step. Numerous are those who have made that step joyfully—in theory, at least.

But I am not sure that they are not wrong in drawing this conclusion, even from their own premises. These premises themselves are in my opinion vitiated by the most serious of errors. They are based on a tragic confusion: the individual is not created for the community; the community exists—and more particularly community in its political aspect—merely to allow the individual, the "person", to pursue and to realise fully his own ends.

But even when we start from these erroneous premises, the conclusion does not seem to me to be exclusively expressed by the word "autarky". The totalitarian state pursues certain ends: power, strength, prestige, perhaps conquest or hegemony, which doubtless, in practice, it puts before many other considerations. Yet, like every other state, it also seeks, without a doubt, prosperity, economic equilibrium, wealth—and all the enhancement that these things may give to the prestige of the leaders internally, and of the régime abroad.

If it were proved that these objects, that is to say prosperity, power, economic independence, could be attained by a policy of effective and complete autarky, there is no doubt that it would soon be carried into effect; it would correspond perfectly to the "climate" of the totalitarian state. To be frank, moreover, let us recognise that if it were so—if it were really possible to assure the economic prosperity and independence of peoples by an autarkic policy —the group of the supporters of international trade would vanish like snow in the sun. The difficulties inherent in commerce carried on under a régime as anarchic as that of international society to-day are tremendous; they would very soon cast into the shade all considerations of culture, sentiment or humani-

4

tarian morality which might still militate in the opposite direction.

Under this hypothesis, the democratic states would not be the last to precipitate themselves into the paths of autarky. If you doubted this, you would have only to cast a glance at the unending list of measures taken by the various states in their endeavours, in the most clumsily egotistic spirit, to shift on to others the load of their difficulties during the last crisis. No state has anything for which to envy or to reproach its neighbours—totalitarian states, democratic states, and even those that do not come within this classification (for there still are some), have to a varying extent fallen into the same mistakes.

But, be that as it may, autarky does not permit the attainment of the objects which we have just mentioned. In reality, autarky is nowhere put into application. Where the policy followed is animated by more or less distinct tendencies in that direction, the latter arise from empirical considerations. In certain cases, they are the logical outcome of a series of errors committed for years, economically or financially; they represent an effort to limit the damage, to defend reserves reduced to a dangerously low level, or to postpone the time of reckoning.

I remember a particularly striking talk which I had with one of these leaders. Here is roughly what he said: "I do not like autarky. I do not believe in it. I should like to import; we need it. But our customers no longer take our products; the gold reserves that we still have do not represent four months' food supply for the country. We cannot take such a risk. We have to fall back on ourselves. It is because we can do nothing better; that is how it is!"

In other cases these autarkic measures do not correspond to a peculiar conception of the economic interest of the state concerned but are simply the threshold of war economics. We cannot but recognise the fact—such, at present, is the character of most of the attempts at autarky. Great countries are specifically organising themselves as if they were in a state of war; the concepts of economic yield or of cost price are overruled by other considerations bearing directly or indirectly on preparation for war, in particular by those of supplies and armament.

But in all cases, these autarkic measures are a source of economic diminution and impoverishment. They entail a fall in the standard of living. They result in products of which the quality is inferior or the "economic" cost price (and not merely the "financial") is higher. Such are facts which are not seriously contested. Those who extol these methods know what they are doing, what these methods imply, what they cost. If these people persist, it is with a knowledge of the facts, because they consider that the price paid is in proportion to the ends pursued, and these ends have no connection with the question of improving the present economic situation of their country.

Be that as it may, even in the countries where the will to autarky has expressed itself in words and decrees, realities have retained the mastery; external relations have continued, because they have had to continue. So, when we adopt the standpoint, not of immediate preparation for war, but of fruitful organisation of the national economic system within the framework of peace, the problem—above and apart from political ideologies—presents itself thus: international economic relations are indispensable; their extent is still considerable to-day, but they are difficult and uncertain; they develop themselves in a disorderly fashion; they have to be regulated, improved, developed, for the benefit of all, outside of any ideological contentions. The question is: How?

The fact is that this task, even when approached with the maximum of good will, is appallingly intricate and complicated. It is not without justification that so many international barriers have been set up on all sides. Even to-day it is not without motives that the leaders hesitate to embark upon an adventure of which we should not minimise the difficulties nor the implications, which are many. To succeed even to a limited extent in this enterprise, it is essential to conceive of a solution complying with the rightful desires of all concerned, taking into account their legitimate considerations, and avoiding the substitution of unknown difficulties for a known difficulty.

Let us then examine the reasons which may keep nations and their leaders in this attitude of hesitation, expectancy or semi-hostility. It is probably in this way that we shall best see what the eventual solution must be, or at least how we may approach it.

## B. DIFFICULTIES INHERENT IN INTERNATIONAL ECONOMIC RELATIONS

### (1) *The Need to develop Trade in both directions*

The first condition to be satisfied in order for an expansion of international economic relations to be possible is that the attempt shall be subordinated to "fair play". Each must be convinced of the necessity of developing international trade in both directions. That means that each participant must desire to see both his exports and his imports develop.

Here I ask many supporters of international liberalism to face the facts honestly. When they extol their theories are they not thinking principally, if not exclusively, of new markets for their products? It is quite legitimate. But to these exports there must be an offset. Now there is in reality only one possible offset, namely the importing of goods or of services. All other offsetting elements play only a provisional part. That is particularly true of gold transfers or international loans. They only defer the problem. When they are used in the right way—in order to spread more easily over a period of time the completion of equilibrium, between two or more national economic systems—that is quite in order; the final solution remains the same, but it is easier to achieve.

But, if the means are mistaken for the end—if it is believed that gold transfers or loans dispense for good and all with the need of imports in order to balance exports—then one is riding for a fall. These means are then diverted from their function, and render the solution more difficult, not more easy; there is a danger that they will result in monetary disturbances, for instance, or in defaults.

In the arguments—of unequal value—that have sometimes been outlined to me in the endeavour to justify or explain unilateral decisions taken by certain great countries, I have heard the following statement recurring like a tag: "They would like to force us to pay and they refuse to accept what we have to give, that is to say, our products!..." What is the answer to that? I know of none.

I am well aware of all the observations that may be formulated; I am sure that several of you have already formulated in your minds the objection that if these products are no longer accepted it is because they are of bad quality, or too expensive. Others say to themselves: "All right, but who began to close the markets, to raise barriers, and so on?..."

But what is the use, what is the point of these bitter remarks? The important thing is not to establish responsibilities, it is to solve a practical problem as it presents itself to us to-day. We must remember this: when leaders of nations want to be sure that the wave of international trade, if it begins to break, will not do so in one direction only, nor in conditions evidently unequal, they are animated by a legitimate care. This being so, all those concerned must, at all stages of negotiation, keep unceasingly before their minds this first truth, a matter of simple common sense, but essential: imports and exports must proceed equally, and as much importance must be attached to one as to the other.

(2) *Repercussions upon the International Economic System of Modifications of Industrial Structure*

Now it is by no means easy to regulate movements of international trade so as to take practical account of this first rule. The disorder we are faced with dates from the last depression. It was then that countries contrived, each one for itself, to find new methods, of which the unavowed object was to pass the difficulty on to its neighbour.

However, the depression is not the real cause; it was only the occasion for this outpouring of protectionist measures, in the worst sense of the word. The cause is elsewhere; it lies in profound modifications of the economic and social structure on which the mutual relations of men are based.

New techniques have revolutionised material conditions of production and the exchange of goods in general. Quite a different attitude of mind has been adopted both by the masses and by statesmen towards the problems of redistributing the wealth of the community. New ideological currents have reversed the order of the values assigned in large communities to material possessions and to moral and psychological advantages. In short, both from the economic and from the social and political point of view the basic conditions of international economic relations have been modified.

Add to these general considerations the changes that have occurred in the respective positions of the different peoples: transformation of the map of Europe, creation of manifold frontiers, birth of new economic entities, transformation of debtor economies into creditor economies, displacement of colonial equilibrium. Who then could be surprised that we are faced to-day with a general problem that is entirely new, and for which many of the former solutions are inadequate* and even apt to be misleading?

## (3) *Fundamental Inequalities in conditions of Competition*

One difficulty of first importance lies in the fundamental inequality in conditions of competition. The progress of means of transport has brought peoples nearer together, but in numerous cases it has also "brought their differences closer together"—if I may so put it—so that the latter are more in conflict instead of

* Without going beyond my subject I cannot further elaborate this point, the importance of which is, however, essential. These ideas have been developed in a book that has recently appeared, entitled *Revision de Valeurs*, and of which I regret that no English translation has so far been published.

diminishing or of dovetailing into each other. This inequality of competition arises sometimes from profound differences in standards of living; sometimes from a very great inequality of capital resources, or again, of raw materials available.

None of these inequalities is to be held, in my view, as a permanent reason for obstructing international economic relations. I would say, on the contrary, that it is by multiplying these relations, in their normal state, that such differences will tend to be levelled—the levelling taking place not from below but from above, that is to say, in a wave of general prosperity.

But the very existence of these inequalities involves a certain number of inevitable consequences. Let us recognise that, temporarily at least, or, if you prefer, in temporary policies, they have constituted a practical obstacle to measures for expanding international trade. This reaction is understandable and legitimate in leaders who are confronted by unforeseen difficulties, and who are meeting the most urgent matters first; it explains many measures to impose quotas, limit imports, refuse payments abroad, and so on. If we want to accomplish something practical, we shall therefore have to take this into account in working out the eventual solution.

## (4) *The need to Provide a Sufficient Period for Adjustment*

Here a rule of procedure makes itself evident, the practical importance of which will become predominant: it is the necessity of guaranteeing to the different markets which will have to adjust themselves to new conditions, a sufficient period for the manœuvre to be carried through without disorder, with the minimum of waste, and paying the least price for the advantages expected from the new policy.

Is he right or wrong, the statesman who, as he begins cautiously to open the door of his market, stops, and thinks of the risk of seeing vast quantities of products come in, manufactured by foreign labour living under conditions of inconceivable misery? Taking a long view, he is wrong. If you admit the legitimacy of international competition, you must accept the normal consequences, whatever they may be. Naturally, the competition must be a loyal one. Nothing is more difficult than to determine *a priori*, in theory, what is a loyal and what is a disloyal competition. In practice, the distinction is much easier to make. Those concerned, when they have the courage to remain objective, rarely make a mistake.

So let us put aside the possibility of dumping. When there is dumping, it is clear that every state has the right and the duty to protect itself, and for myself I consider it legitimate to give to the word "dumping" a wide interpretation, covering the manifold forms, as ingenious as they are regrettable, that it may adopt. But from the moment that dumping is excluded, it must be admitted that, if other countries produce more cheaply than you, whatever may be the reasons for it, their products are rightly outdoing other products.

The countries most advanced socially must find means to counterbalance the cheapness of labour in less civilised countries. They can do so thanks to many advantages: to more abundant capital, to more highly developed technique, and to wider knowledge. Under a régime of international division of labour, the richest and the most advanced must assume the most complicated tasks; they must accordingly consent to readapt themselves gradually in order to meet these transformations.

But such reasoning, logical though it may be, is principally of value on a long reckoning. The immediate acceptance of these principles, without reserve or transition, would expose the national economic system to the risk of upset. Time is necessary to transfer a whole population of workers from one industry to another. There are, besides, invested capital, acquired rights; time is necessary to liquidate them, partially at least. Violent shocks would be liable to bring about unemployment and waste of capital.

We must then, in practice, admit that those who make demands for moderation, assurances, time to adapt themselves, are in the right. The essential thing is that the policy chosen, even if it is a slow one, should be turned in the right direction. It matters little whether the adapting takes a little longer or a little shorter time, *provided that it is carried out.*

## (5) *Legitimate Concern for National Security and for Economic and Social Stability*

The care for the development of material wealth, of national revenue, of the assets in general placed at the disposal of the community—such is and such remains the principal motive for business, economic activity, and international trade. But let us not lose sight of the fact that other preoccupations may override this care, even in the economic domain, or at any rate on its frontiers. The desire for material security, the determination to preserve a certain economic stability, often prevail over the consideration of increasing the volume of wealth to be distributed.

If you were faced yourselves with the dilemma either of giving employment to the whole working class of your country, with a final return of 90 per cent, or to two-thirds of it, leaving the rest unemployed, with a final return of 100 per cent, which solution would you choose? For my part, I should not hesitate; before the disastrous consequences of unemployment, in the social and moral sphere and in its economic repercussions themselves—deterioration of the technical qualities of labour, increased rigidity, and so forth—I should not hesitate an instant to choose the first. I am well aware that things never do present themselves with this conciseness or this simplicity. But such a presentation, schematic though it may be, nevertheless corresponds to realities; it evokes the problem which is set before the leaders of many countries, and throws light on their state of mind.

## (6) *Other Aspects of the Problem*

To this enumeration of difficulties we must add the claims formulated with respect to the international economic system by a set of countries who judge themselves unfairly treated: access to raw materials, maldistribution of capital, repartition of colonies, settling of international debts—so many friction points which might easily get worse. To whatever extent these claims may or may not be justifiable, they must be taken as a fact, and the real psychological obstacle that they constitute must be removed.

Certain of these claims, moreover, are connected with fundamental problems of which the solution is imperative, if it is desired to set, on lasting bases, the sought-for reorganisation. I will mention only one of these problems, but an important one, with all its implications: the international money problem, the reform of the gold standard, the relations of currencies to each other and to gold, international movements of capital and, in particular, of short-term capital.

## III

# EXAMINATION OF A PRACTICAL METHOD TOWARDS REALISATION

## A. A MODERATE SOLUTION

Having reached this point in my exposé, I wonder whether I have not unduly alarmed you. Certain of you must have the impression that the problem is so complicated and involved, so intimately bound up with social, moral and political questions, so heavily overruled by contradictory interests and feelings or by inveterate situations, that its solution must be a titanic task, if not an impossible one.

If this were the case, I should have exceeded my object. Certainly the problem is difficult to settle—most difficult. It arises in conditions so new that the examples of the past are no longer of much use to us. No solution has a hope of being admitted unless it avoids the dangers or meets the numerous objections that we have pointed out. But we have an ally, a most powerful ally: necessity. Doubtless that is not enough. But it gives us a solid base to work on. Besides, there is no lack of supporting factors, or of favourable elements. Finally, we have drawn certain lessons from former failure; they have not all been in vain.

Here I am obliged to speak to you of the Report which I have handed to the British and French governments, and even to defend its suggestions, at least in their essence. I in no way consider the suggestions made in this Report as forming the Solution, with a capital S. Many other means than these may be conceived to attain the object. Certain of the suggestions made have already, moreover, been outdistanced by events. Nevertheless, I believe that the arguments on which the Report is based, the general direction that it indicates, and the possibilities contained in the method advocated, are more actual and urgent than ever.

First, it seems to me that one must not be too ambitious; the examination we have made of the difficulties of the problem show how wise it is to take the situation such as it is to-day, and to begin by preventing its worsening. If we could only succeed in preventing further advance along the path of protectionism, it would already be quite an achievement. If we could succeed in removing from international affairs the element of confusion constituted by continual modifications of tariffs, nomenclatures, and regulations, it would surely not be negligible. Furthermore, the very moderation of the suggestions put forward would permit satisfaction to be given, in many cases, to the concern for internal stability that rightly animates so many national leaders.

I should like no mistake to be made, however, as to the real nature of my thought. I have reached the conclusion that in the matter of international economic relations it is necessary to proceed at this moment, and for reasons above all pragmatic, slowly and with extreme caution. Do not deduce from this that I also apply this spirit to the ensemble of the problems of economic reorganisation. Quite the contrary. Profound changes are in process; greater ones will perhaps reveal themselves necessary before long. We have not yet "digested" the discoveries which have revolutionised the field of industrial technique; we have not yet succeeded in incorporating them into a social and economic organisation presenting the characters of a lasting equilibrium; *a fortiori*, we have not yet adapted the political forms of the modern state to these changes of economic structure.

Along that line, we have no longer the time to act slowly. We ought to move quickly and resolutely. "Do not stand and watch the transformations of your age go past", said Albert de Mun, "with the resignation of the conquered; climb boldly into the convoy and try to steer the machine."

To make my thought clear, let me just take, as examples, one or two of these problems of to-day or of to-morrow. How shall we assure equilibrium between a production with infinitely increased possibilities, and a consumption which is both its condition and its object? If this problem, as I believe, comes down to assuring equilibrium between the different forms of production, how is this equilibrium to be established between "capitalist" production industries and "final" consumption industries? How shall we restore to the tasks of production their human aspect, their "personalism"? How shall we rid production of its parasites, without impairing its suppleness and its adaptability? How shall we bring about this necessary evolution without compromising the rise of any social group, without giving up any of the "reasons for living" that we find in our "humanist" civilisation?

That the answer to these problems interests the whole of humanity is self-evident. The real solidarity—in error as in success—that unites the nations of the earth is not on the decline; quite the contrary; the material *rapprochement* which arises from the improvement in methods of transport is an important element in it. Suppose that great countries give to the economic or political problems of the moment separate and individual solutions, proper to themselves alone; we can immediately see the consequences that result for the rest of the world; the part that Germany and Italy have been playing in the last few years is a glaring proof of it.

It seems then that these problems also, the range of which extends to the community of nations closely interdependent, ought to be solved in a spirit of international collaboration. In the present condition of the world, however, and in view of the far-reaching disorganisation of international life, I believe that the essential tasks of this economic, social and political re-organisation will have to be accomplished first in the national field. It is only at a later stage that the inferences may be drawn on an international scale.

## B. THE URGENCY OF THE PROBLEM

We must for the moment, I think, by force of circumstances, if we do not want to run into a wall and break ourselves against it, limit our ambitions in the international field, and refer to it only the problems that are essential for the development of international trade. Even in this limited domain, we shall have to satisfy ourselves with moderate and empirical solutions—for a start. But this task is extremely urgent. Let it be begun from *any* direction; whether it is better tacked on to political negotiations, or whether the political difficulty is better obviated by approaching straightway the economic problem, all that is unimportant. But one cannot, without danger, let the evil become ingrained.

For myself, I have reached the urgent conviction that we must go into action without more delay. My reasons are these. The solutions indicated in the Report are all of them inspired by a desire for "fair play" towards all countries, whatever they may be. It is possible, I think—and at least we should try—to make a start with the reorganising of international economic relations without asking anyone to show his credentials, to renounce or to modify any ideological positions. If this result—modest but of capital importance—could be attained, humanity would not be "saved from the waters", but a cause of friction would have been suppressed, and opportunities of lasting *rapprochement* would have been created.

In so far as international order might thus be established and so promote prosperity and material progress, it would facilitate the settling of the remaining difficulties. Prosperity functions as oil in an engine; it is not the oil that makes the engine run; if this or that part of it is missing, the engine will not run, even if you drown it in oil; but without oil it will not run for long; it will get hot and finally stop—unless it blows up!

To-day I do not see any better, more direct or more effective way of working to increase the chance of peace or to lessen the risk of war—whichever you prefer—than to facilitate the material task of the great states by re-establishing order in the domain of international economics.

## C. WHENCE CAN COME THE INITIATIVE?

You will at once object that, for an understanding to be reached, for a compromise to be set up, there must exist on all sides at least the intention to try. What is the present situation? This intention exists without a doubt in the great democracies, the United States, England and France.

I am not empowered to commit anyone. No one, during the enquiry that we have conducted, has ever adopted any *a priori* position from which the slightest commitment, moral or otherwise, might be drawn. In speaking, as I am at this moment, as an ordinary citizen, I am expressing only a personal opinion. But the gestures made repeatedly by the governments of these three countries, the consideration that urged upon them the mission with which I was charged, the official statements of many of their leading statesmen—all these things allow us to conclude that in those quarters good will exists, even if circumstances keep it latent.

Let us look round the other countries of Europe or America whose economic rôle is important; in the majority of cases, you will find the same desire to do something—a desire which would rapidly assume a constructive form if the great powers took an initiative.

There remain the countries with a totalitarian régime: What would Germany do? Or Italy? What would Russia do? What is their real attitude? I have told you why I consider neither totalitarian ideology, nor declarations tending to autarky, as insurmountable obstacles to international economic action.

It must, however, be recognised that the last few months have not been favourable: no gesture has been made to give the slightest indication of a desire for constructive *rapprochement* on economic ground. Is this a reason for not acting? No, on the contrary.

Let us suppose an initiative taken to-morrow. Whether that initiative follows entirely or in part the suggestions I have outlined, or whether it takes a different course, is of little importance, provided that it takes into account all the elements of the problem and that it springs from the same concern for "fair play" towards all, without exception.

By whom could such an initiative be taken?

Let us consider possibilities. Let us imagine this gesture made by the four powers whose leaders sat together at Munich recently. Do you doubt for a moment that the other countries of the world would fall into line and associate themselves in the search for an arrangement from which, by definition, each would stand to benefit?

Let us consider another possibility. Suppose that President Roosevelt, whose boldness and foresight have been revealed by his recent messages, decides to take up the reins once more. Let us suppose that some other very eminent leader, of a small country, takes the risk of the initiative, for the sake of peace, in a spirit of mediation. Do you not believe that the effect on the others might be decisive?

Let us go on, in our supposition. Let us suppose that England and France take the first steps, that they send an invitation to the others, summoning them to the same rights and the same duties. What would happen? Is it exaggerated to believe that under present circumstances the immense majority of nations would respond to such a call?

But we must consider a possible check: what

would be the result if one or other great power refused to take a place round the common table? It would be a profoundly disturbing sign; but let us face the difficulty squarely. Is it absolutely necessary that all, without any exception, agree to the scheme beforehand, in order to go ahead, and initiate something? Or, would it not be advisable to begin with a large majority, if the unanimity cannot be obtained, and to show enough good will to induce the others to join rapidly? For the agreement eventually contracted by a number of powers would, according to my views, remain essentially open to all. The place of the absentees would remain marked. The invitation to join the group would be permanent. On the day that they changed their attitude, they would be received as cordially as if they were amongst the first-hour workers.

Is it excessive to hope that the advantages reaped by those forming part of the organised group would be obvious enough, after a certain time, to induce the absentees to re-examine their attitude? Of course, such a reasoning remains stubbornly established upon the one moral basis: namely, that a minimum of good will, and specifically a sufficient desire for peace, shall continue to animate all powers, whether or not they take an immediate part in the effort towards international economic organisation. If it were to be otherwise, if it were established that certain powers are deliberately setting aside all the elements of a peace economy to enter upon a war economy, these last hopes would vanish, but it would be one more reason for going ahead with economic organisation, amongst all of good will.

# CONCLUSION

Such is the opinion which I believed I could and must express before you to-day. Was it the right moment? I fully realise how far the atmosphere that we have been breathing in Europe for weeks and months is explosive. Any constructive suggestion, any proposal tending to modify positions that have been adopted, is liable to be wrongly interpreted on one side or the other; or, more serious still, there is a great danger of it being foundered beneath the weight of an inertia which no longer results from mere indifference, but from a sort of fatalistic resignation to the worst. Yet the disproportion between the risk of war and any other difficulty, any other drawback whatsoever, is such that everything really deserves to be tried.

For myself, and this I beg you to take as my conclusion, I am convinced that material prosperity, that economic progress, are permanent elements that weigh in the scales of peace. I believe that a reorganisation of international economic relations, under the sign of expansion, of adaptation, of order, would favour the prosperity of the commonwealth of nations; it would facilitate the re-establishment of an internal equilibrium in certain countries which at present are up against great difficulties; I believe that for all economic problems arising between nations there can be found solutions showing a considerable profit balance for each and for all. Hence I consider that the chance must be given to this generation. The moment has come, not because external events have rendered the task more easy—alas, one might contest any such assertion—but because they contain within themselves imminent perils, to which all possible resistance must be opposed.

Nothing can be done if great powers, whose destiny it is to be at the head, do not take the initiative. My dearest wish is that this initiative should be taken soon, and that Britain should once more play a decisive part—that directing rôle which she is trying so often to cast far from her, and which destiny continues with no less insistence to place upon her shoulders.

Thank Heaven, British policy is to a large extent the policy formed by the opinion, the free opinion, of the British people. If I make no mistake, that opinion is asserting itself calmly, with reserve and caution but with strength, in ways that answer several of the wishes that have just been expressed. If this is so, we can look to the future with more confidence.

Perhaps we had fallen very low? But I like to remember with Shakespeare himself:

*Some falls are means the happier to arise.*

Whatever may be the bitterness and the doubt that numberless deceptions have left in the hearts of men; whatever may be the dangers that still threaten us and the trials through which we must still pass; let me quote to you, as a final wish and as a sign of hope, a splendid sentence of the great French scientist, Pasteur:

*I believe invincibly that knowledge and peace will triumph over ignorance and war; that the nations will come to an understanding, not to destroy, but to build, and that the future will belong to those who will have done the most to relieve the sufferings of mankind.*

www.ingramcontent.com/pod-product-compliance
Ingram Content Group UK Ltd.
Pitfield, Milton Keynes, MK11 3LW, UK
UKHW042141280225
455719UK00001B/3